Original title:
Tassels and Truth

Copyright © 2025 Creative Arts Management OÜ
All rights reserved.

Author: Julian Montgomery
ISBN HARDBACK: 978-1-80586-225-3
ISBN PAPERBACK: 978-1-80586-697-8

Braided Realities

In a world where knots dance free,
Strings of laughter twist with glee.
Fabrics tangle, colors collide,
Who knew a mess could hold such pride?

Yarns are spun with tales so bold,
A patchwork quilt of stories told.
Life's a tapestry, bright and bizarre,
Stitching quirks like a shooting star.

The Fabric of Existence

Life's a quilt with mismatched squares,
Threaded memories, silly affairs.
Frogs in hats and dancing cats,
Craziness woven in the chats.

Is it real or just a dream?
A spinning top, a whizzing beam.
Whimsical threads, a jolly spree,
The fabric stretches, just let it be.

Unraveled Secrets

Underneath a warm cocoon,
Hide the giggles, peek at the moon.
Each unravel reveals a smile,
Secrets wink, just stay awhile.

Stitches slip, oh what a riot,
Bumbles and fumbles, let's not fight it.
Knit together with bright hues of fun,
No more hiding, let's all run!

Ornate Illusions

Illusions dance on fabric seams,
Where nothing is quite as it seems.
Twirling hats and frilly ties,
Crafting giggles, oh what a guise!

A table set with forks of cheese,
Cooking up mishaps, if you please.
Colors clash, yet hold a cheer,
In this bizarre world, do persevere!

Twine of Transparency

In knots we find a crafty game,
They twist and turn, a funny name.
With every loop, a laughter's sprout,
Truth hangs low, but hangs about.

The threads we tangle, round and round,
In messy schemes, our joy is found.
Each color bright, a story told,
Laughter's warmth breaks through the cold.

We tie the shoe, we tie the bow,
Yet still we trip, oh where to go?
In playful banter, we trip and sway,
Who knew the truth could dance this way?

So grab a strand, let's make a mess,
With joy and giggles, we'll confess.
For in each twist, there's laughter brewing,
What's real may wobble, but is worth pursuing.

In the Twists and Turns

Oh, how we spin with gleeful flair,
It's like a circus, soaring through air.
With every twist, we laugh and spin,
In life's big game, we all win.

The path we take, a loop-de-loop,
Like jumping frogs in a silly troupe.
Truths hide under clowns with ease,
They tumble out, just laugh and tease.

A winding road, a fumble here,
But oh, the joy outweighs the fear.
Each little bobble, a dance of sorts,
In our jesting world, the silliness courts.

So come along on this merry ride,
With giggles and chuckles, side by side.
Forget the straight lines and adhere to fun,
In turns and twists, we burst like the sun.

The Loom of Sincerity

In the workshop, yarns entwined,
Laughter dances, truth unconfined.
A stitch gone wrong, a color clash,
Fabrications bring a vibrant splash.

The weaver's tale, a tangled thread,
Whispers secrets that can't be said.
With every knot, a story brews,
In fabric fun, the joke ensues.

Pendulous Paradoxes

Swinging low, the fabric sways,
Contradictions weave in playful ways.
A truth that bends like silly string,
Makes you laugh, oh what a fling!

Each yarn a riddle, twists in air,
With blunders bold, we reach for flair.
A pendulum of sense and jest,
Where nonsense wears the truth's fine vest.

Knotted Narratives

Tales get tangled, loops and swirls,
A world of giggles, twists and twirls.
Each knot a secret, tied with glee,
In this absurdity, we're all free.

Characters popping, threads unite,
Woven in humor, oh what a sight!
A plot that hops, perplexity grows,
In knotted tales, hilarity flows.

Dangled Certainty

On the edge, where laughter hangs,
Certainty jiggles, prances and flangs.
Each dangling truth, a playful tease,
Swinging around, as we laugh with ease.

A zest for life, so bright and clear,
Where laughter chimes, there's nothing to fear.
Hanging by threads, we float and sway,
In this dance of fools, we jest all day.

The Hidden Patterns of Self

In the closet, secrets hide,
Unraveled threads do abide.
With every color, a tale to weave,
What will they say, if I believe?

Shirts that speak in tones of glee,
Pants that prance, oh can't you see?
Patterns clash with quite a flair,
Can't wear this? Oh, do I care?

Bound by the Beaded Edge

Beads are charming, a shiny lot,
But wait, these pants? A fashion blot!
Jingling all as I take a stride,
Their echoing laughs? I cannot hide.

Sunlight hits like a crown on my hat,
While beads roll off, just like that.
A merry dance in a quirky line,
Each jingle drowns my sense of time.

Sinews of Clarity Within Chaos

In the room, chaos reigns supreme,
Socks mismatched, what a dream!
Ribbons tangle, oh what a sight,
Lost my keys? Might be right!

Every corner, a twist of fate,
Laundry piles create a great state.
Through the ruckus, a laugh erupts,
Finding fun where clutter disrupts.

A Raiment of Unveiled Light

Draped in fabric, light as air,
Daring patterns? I don't care!
Twinkling threads dance in delight,
Wearing whimsy feels just right.

Each swish and sway, a giggle grows,
Garments whisper their silly prose.
In a world that often masks,
I choose to shine, no need for tasks.

Amidst the Glistening

Beneath the shimmer, secrets hide,
Laughter dances, like a tide.
Ribbons waving, tales unfold,
Witty wonders, bright and bold.

Fanciful fables, spun with care,
Knots of nonsense fill the air.
Each flicker shines, a jest in play,
Chasing shadows, come what may.

The Stitch of Epiphany

In a patchwork quilt of life's surprise,
Needles poke, and wisdom lies.
Sewing stories with a grin,
Every stitch where laughs begin.

Unraveled thoughts, they twist and twirl,
Jumbled fabric starts to whirl.
A seam here, a snip right there,
Finding humor everywhere.

Shredded Realities

Strapped in laughter, time's a prank,
Paper-thin floors at the prankster's bank.
Reality's threads begin to fray,
In this world, odd rules hold sway.

Confetti dreams on the ground fall,
Witty whispers, we hear them call.
Life's a comedy, sharp as a knife,
Shredded moments, oh what a life!

Revelations of the Ornate

Curls of gold in a grand display,
Glimmers wink, and jesters play.
Laced with humor, rich and wide,
Jovial munchkins by our side.

Ornate schemes in a playful jest,
Each reveal is a witty test.
With each flourish, giggles bloom,
Laughter erupts in the fanciest room.

Twisted Vows

In a chapel made of twine,
The vows were held in line.
One promised cakes and pies,
While the other winked with eyes.

They spoke of love in rhymes,
With laughter, they played chimes.
But every word was spun,
As they danced and laughed for fun.

With bated breath, they signed,
But plans were swiftly twined.
Instead of rings, there came socks,
And laughter echoed in the flocks.

Fabricated Echoes

In a room of jesters' games,
We whispered half-truths with names.
A sound of giggles filled the air,
As secrets tangoed without a care.

The tales were spun like yarn,
Each twist held a charm.
With every chuckle, hearts grew light,
As echoes danced into the night.

A fib about a chubby cat,
Who wore a hat, now imagine that!
As each truth morphed with a grin,
Fabrications grew and curled within.

Delicate Revelations

A revelation took its flight,
In a fabric shop of delight.
She revealed her plans ahead,
To sew her secrets with no thread.

Each patch held a little joke,
With every stitch, a yoke.
But when she slipped and fell with glee,
The only truth was fabric free.

A friend exclaimed, 'What a tear!',
As laughter wove into the air.
Underneath those woven lies,
Were delicate truths in disguise.

Curious Ribbons

With ribbons tied in knots and bows,
A mystery that's fun, who knows?
Each color held a tale so bright,
Of candy dreams and sleepless nights.

Curious ones gathered 'round,
As silly stories did abound.
In the shuffle of satin twirl,
The giggles brought a joyful whirl.

When one spoke of a fee for mail,
The ribbons danced with every detail.
In ribbons, truths began to mingle,
Leaving all with a cheerful jingle.

Garlands of Clarity

In a land where notions twine,
Knotted thoughts take time to shine.
Each loop a laugh, each flick a jest,
We ponder on, yet never rest.

Colors clash, and styles collide,
The fashion sense we cannot hide.
With bright ideas tied so tight,
We trip on wisdom, quite a sight!

The strings of wit dangle and sway,
With every word, we lead astray.
A playful twist, a cheeky grin,
In this wild game, where do we begin?

So wear your garland, smile wide,
Let nonsense be your joyful guide.
For clarity in a tangled mess,
Is the secret to most happiness!

The Ornament of Intent

A bauble bright upon my shelf,
Reflects the wish to be myself.
But how it wobbles, here and there,
Intentions fly on floating air!

Dangled thoughts, like ornaments hang,
With synthetic joy, they make us sang.
Unruly choices bob and roll,
In this mad dance, we find our soul.

Polish it up, the sparkles gleam,
Crafting life as if a dream.
Yet all this nonsense, all this flair,
Just laughter spun in sunny air!

So wear that ornament with pride,
And let your inner child collide.
For in this chaos, pure delight,
Intentions twirl in cheerful flight!

Primed Chaos

In a room where jesters play,
Ideas dance in disarray.
Spinning thoughts like tops on floor,
Each one crashes, begging more!

What's primed today, who can decipher?
Wit's mischief carved, daily splicer.
A joke unfolds, and then a twist,
In the current of life, how can we resist?

Colors burst, as paint does splatter,
Thoughts collide, and laughter's matter.
In this circus of the absurd,
A bumble bee's a singing bird!

So embrace the chaos, let it reign,
For laughter rides on every train.
In this mad house, let's enjoy the flaws,
Chaos primed, a round of applause!

Textured Reality

Reality's a fabric spun,
With threads of laughter, jokes for fun.
Tangled fibers make us grin,
Where nonsense hides, let joy begin!

A patchwork quilt of wild delight,
Each square a story, bright and light.
Textures woven, bumps and grooves,
In this wild ride, we find our moves.

From cotton candy clouds we dream,
To layers of an ice cream theme.
We scoop the flavors, mix and match,
A textured dance, a dandy patch!

So dive into this vibrant field,
Where nonsense, mirth, and truth are healed.
In every stitch, a chuckle dwells,
In textured realms, our heart repels!

The Fringe Beneath

In a world where fray meets cheer,
A quirky edge, oh so dear.
Threads of laughter, colors bright,
Dancing merrily in the light.

With a twirl and a little jig,
Sudden spills could make you gig.
But those who trip on strings so neat,
Find joy in tumbles on their feet.

Frayed edges tell a tale or two,
Of daring adventures, wild and new.
A missing bead, a slipping clasp,
Life's little hiccups make us laugh.

So let's embrace the silly side,
Where stitches pop and seams collide.
In every knot, a giggle sneaks,
In every join, a chuckle peeks.

Woven Confessions

In the fabric of our days,
Fibers twist in funny ways.
Secrets woven, tangled tight,
Disguised within a silly sight.

When a scarf wraps 'round too fast,
You'll find yourself in quite the grasp.
One wrong pull, it's quite a scene,
A comedy of threads unseen.

Each loop a story, fraught with glee,
Knitted flaws that set us free.
With every pattern, yarn is spun,
Chasing laughs, we've just begun.

So here's to patterns, wild and bright,
Each yarn a laugh, each twist a delight.
In stitches soaring, life's a play,
Woven confessions, come what may!

Looming Shadows

In the shadows that we cast,
Patterns emerge, fun and vast.
With each sway of fabric light,
Absurd shapes come into sight.

A silhouette of socks gone rogue,
Mismatched pairs that oddly vogue.
Echoes of laughter as one falls,
A wiggly dance in wall's tall halls.

Fringes waving, obscure and grand,
Tickling toes as they take a stand.
The absurdity's the clever guise,
In every patch, a sweet surprise.

So let's not fret if things get frayed,
In tangled moments, joy is made.
For in our foibles, bright and bold,
Looming shadows, stories told.

Adornments of Authenticity

A brooch that's lost its shiny grace,
Still holds a quirky, charming face.
A silly wink from mismatched flair,
Life's little gems on every wear.

Necklaces tangled in a twist,
Fashion faux pas you can't resist.
With a laugh, we wear our style,
Embracing flaws that spark a smile.

Earrings bouncing, dancing free,
A mismatched pair, such glee to see.
In every choice, truth wears a grin,
Adorned in laughter, let's begin.

So gather 'round the fun we make,
In every wobbly move we take.
For in our quirks, we find the gold,
Adornments bright, our stories told.

The Charm of Contradictions

In a world where socks don't match,
The cat wears a hat, a fine catch.
Birds that speak in solemn tones,
While fish just laugh in silly groans.

Giraffes sipping tea, quite absurd,
Play chess with turtles, quite a herd.
The wise owl dances, full of glee,
With penguins who waltz in the sea.

Lions in pajamas sip on juice,
Debating the merits of moose on a truce.
Dogs trade secrets with the mailman,
While toads recite poetry, a grand plan.

Unicorns prance in roller skates,
While wise old frogs give dating rates.
Life's a stage with mishaps so bright,
Embrace the chaos, it feels just right.

Ebbing Illusions

The toaster sings when bread's not there,
While socks conspire under the chair.
Mirrors giggle at their own reflection,
As chairs plot plans for their disconnection.

A moose in a tutu prances around,
While shadows tango without a sound.
Clouds wear sunglasses, act so cool,
While the sun plays tricks, what a duel!

Silly hats tip their brims in jest,
All while the clock takes a peculiar rest.
Roosters that dance, so full of surprise,
While cats send texts, oh what a rise!

The night shifts gears, a curious scheme,
Daring the day to join in the dream.
And laughter echoes in the playhouse of minds,
As reality bends, and mischief unwinds.

The Curved Tapestry

We weave our tales with odd little threads,
Where owls wear glasses and bake their breads.
Kangaroos recite Shakespeare with flair,
And ants hold parties at the tops of stairs.

A wizard with bubble gum in his pocket,
Ties shoelaces up in a tangled locket.
The moon wears boots, stomping around,
While stars hum tunes, so goofy and sound.

Ducks don tuxedos for the grand ball,
And raccoons debate who's best of them all.
With a wink and a nod, each secret unfurls,
As mischief darts through their whimsical swirls.

On this vibrant quilt, odd rules apply,
Like jellybeans soaring through the sky.
Capture the laughter, in every stitch,
Life's a curious blend, a glorious glitch.

Shrouded Enigmas

In a cupboard that's filled with socks of all shades,
A turtle's been plotting elaborate charades.
While the kettle does jiggles, dances and hops,
Raccoons throw parties, on top of the shops.

A fish with a monocle calls for a toast,
While llamas debate what they love the most.
Kettlecorn clouds sprinkle down sweet,
As giants play hopscotch in retrospect's seat.

With shadows that frolic, and whispers that sing,
A mouse rides a bike, oh what a wild fling!
The clock strikes thirteen, and everyone knows,
Time's just a prankster in colorful clothes.

An enigma draped in silly designs,
Where lemons do tango, and ketchup just shines.
In this realm of wonders, where laughter is fierce,
Join in the fun; let your worries disperse.

Emblems of Genuineness in the Breeze

In the wind, they sway and dance,
A colorful bunch, oh what a chance!
To question life with a wiggly grin,
And giggle loud at where we've been.

Fluffy tales in a rustling throng,
Whispering secrets, where we belong.
Each twist and turn, a laugh we find,
In the threads that tie our playful mind.

Bright colors twirl in silly delight,
As we ponder truths in the moonlight.
A jester's cap on a wise old sage,
Foolish riddles on a blank page.

As laughter weaves through tales untold,
We embrace the wobbly antics of old.
For in the breeze, our hearts take flight,
Chasing after joy, morning to night.

The Fringes of Inner Wilderness

Out in the wild, where the critters sigh,
Fringes flap under the bright blue sky.
Chasing shadows, dancing with glee,
Finding truths that tickle, you see.

An otter's caper, a raccoon's grin,
Life's a circus, let the fun begin!
In the tangled shrubs, we laugh and play,
While searching for wisdom in a haystack's sway.

A squirrel with a stash, so full of surprises,
Dropping acorns like little prizes.
Truths tiptoe softly, wearing bright shoes,
Along pathways hidden, we'll always choose.

Amidst the chaos, a giggle breaks free,
Waving at life, come and join me!
For in every corner, laughter may bloom,
In the wild fringes, there's always room.

Threads of Revelation

In the fabric of thoughts that twist and twine,
Little quirks and giggles start to shine.
Come join the ride on this threadbare spree,
Where truth and jest enjoy a cup of tea.

Filaments flutter in a zany spin,
Painting the day with a cheeky grin.
Tales unravel, not quite in line,
But who needs straight when you dine on divine?

Every peek beneath, a jester's jest,
Revealing giggles that pass the test.
In the loom of laughter, we find our place,
Weaving wisdom with a funny face.

Let's unravel knots with a chuckle and cheer,
For the threads of life hold nothing to fear.
Mirth and insight, a colorful blend,
On this fabric of life, let's twist and extend!

Fringes of Clarity

In the blur of life, details may tease,
Revealing clarity with a side of breeze.
Fringes waddle like ducks in a line,
Each one a joke, a nonsensical sign.

Silly whispers in a crowded space,
Riddles and laughs draw smiles on each face.
The light shines bright on the edge of a tale,
As we tumble and giggle, it's never too frail.

Through the haze of nonsense, we stumble on,
Finding wisdom beneath a cheeky yawn.
With each twirl and leap, we shake off the weight,
A joyous conundrum we happily create.

So here's to the moments, silly and clear,
Embracing the fun in the things that appear.
As we dance on the fringes, let laughter ignite,
In the depths of absurd, we find sheer delight.

Haywire Ribbons

In a world of running strings,
Unexpected twists and flings.
Ribbons tied in a clumsy bow,
Laughing at how they love to show.

Every loop a story told,
Funky colors, bright and bold.
Dancing dreams on frayed ends,
Tangled laughter, the best of friends.

Winds may blow, and knots may sway,
But we find joy in the fray.
As chaos reigns in every dance,
We tiptoe through, given a chance.

Oh, the tales each flutter bears,
Each absurd twist, a comedic flair.
We laugh and twirl through life's parade,
In every mishap, joy is made.

The Essence of Strands

A spider spun an awkward web,
Caught up in threads no one can ebb.
Glitter glues and dangling charms,
Life's little quirks bring silly alarms.

Entwined tales of absurd delight,
Mismatched colors that look just right.
Fibers weaving through the air,
Creating chaos with utmost care.

Silly shapes that swirl and twist,
In happy moments that can't be missed.
With every strand, a giggle blooms,
Room for joy amidst the glooms.

So here's to strands that wobble and sway,
For our laughter lights up the way.
In each frayed edge or funky string,
We'll celebrate the joy they bring.

Knots of Understanding

In knots we find the strangest art,
A twist of fate that warms the heart.
What was straight now takes a turn,
In tangled messes, wisdom we learn.

Each knot a tale of laughter shared,
Learning to care when we're ensnared.
Solutions hidden in jumbled parts,
We untie joy with our wobbly hearts.

The more we try to straighten out,
The more we find there's no doubt.
Life's rather funky, bright and bold,
Twisty turns are treasures to hold.

So let's embrace each loop and tie,
In knots of laughter, we'll soar high.
With every twist that comes our way,
We'll find the fun in the fray.

Flamboyant Doubts

In colors bright, questions arise,
Funny hats and silly ties.
Wobbly thoughts march with flair,
Chasing laughter, light as air.

Curly cues that shift and sway,
Doubts in sequins dance and play.
Glimmers of truth in a jest's embrace,
Life's a show, a lively chase.

Each question asks with a wink,
A spin of doubt that makes us think.
With vibrant strokes, we paint our fears,
Turning worries into cheers.

So let's wear hats of quirks and jokes,
Among the laughter, wisdom pokes.
In flamboyant shades, we'll prance about,
Finding joy in every doubt.

Fringed Echoes of Reality

In a room where laughter blooms,
Puffy cushions toss with glee,
A cat lounges with big, bright eyes,
Chasing shadows, wild and free.

Socks mate in a joyful dance,
While the toaster pops with pride,
Each slice of bread a happy chance,
To spread some jam and glide.

Lawn gnomes gossip, take their stand,
In the garden, they plot and scheme,
While squirrels steal away with nuts,
Their little heists, a crazy dream.

As the clock ticks off the day,
Time waltzes with silly cheer,
In this echo of light and play,
Reality twists—oh dear!

Threads of Honesty Unraveled

A pair of shoes with mismatched laces,
Takes its stroll upon the street,
Say hello to the curious faces,
Of happy folks eager to meet.

The toaster mutters sweet nothings,
While the kettle sings a tune,
Spilling secrets of their musings,
Under the watchful gaze of the moon.

In the cupboard, there lies a plan,
To bake a cake with extra sprinkles,
But flour clouds and tiny hands
Result in laughter and comical crinkles.

Every mishap a joyful jest,
Where honesty's the perfect joke,
Life may not always be the best,
But it surely makes us choke!

The Weave Beneath the Surface

In a quilt of quirks and dreams,
Stitching together unlikely themes,
A frog with wings decides to fly,
Buzzing 'round with a cheerful cry.

The curtains dance in a breezy waltz,
With secrets tangled in their folds,
While the mirror smiles at all the faults,
Reflecting stories yet untold.

Underneath the polished sky,
Where laughter floats like paper boats,
A candle flickers with a sigh,
Sharing tales of old-time goats.

The patterns twist in a funny spin,
Reality woven with blushing threads,
Each feature, an accidental grin,
As the sunlight softly spreads.

Knots of Wisdom in the Wind

A kite flies high with a crooked tail,
In windy whispers of life's grand tale,
It dips and dives in the swirling air,
Offering lessons with giddy flair.

Puddles form—a child's delight,
As they leap with all their might,
Splashing stories, laughter shared,
In every jump, they show they cared.

Old trees sway with branches wide,
Knots of stories they cannot hide,
Their leaves laugh softly with the breeze,
Sharing secrets among the trees.

In every twist and playful swirl,
The wisdom that the world can spin,
Reminds us all—without a twirl,
Life's just a giggle in the wind!

Delicate Unravelings of the Heart

A string of dreams hangs low,
Pull it once, watch love's show.
Knots and loops, a dance of fate,
Untangle quick, before it's late.

Laughter's thread is woven tight,
In the daylight, hearts take flight.
Tickles turn to joyful gasps,
With every pull, a new surprise clasps.

Patterns change with every tug,
Warmth and charm inside a mug.
Stitching bits of silly schemes,
We sew our life with happy themes.

Sometimes loose, sometimes a bind,
Each mistake is lovely, just unwind.
In chaos lies a merry spark,
Unravel soft, let laughter embark.

Gilded Hems of Reflection

Shiny edges catch the eye,
Fringed delight in the blink of a tie.
Merriment flows where laughter spills,
Glistening dreams dance on life's hills.

A flick of fabric, so absurd,
We search for meaning in every word.
Sewing patches of silly darts,
Crafted pieces of loving hearts.

Sometimes frayed, sometimes bright,
Every slip brings more delight.
In these threads of life, we cling,
To the joy that each moment can bring.

Gilded tales within the seams,
Reflecting laughter on twisted beams.
As garments spin and twirl around,
A jolly hum is the sweetest sound.

Splayed Furl of Honesty

A twisty truth in fabric wraps,
It giggles softly as it snaps.
Laughter echoes, lies in play,
Whispers of love in the fray.

Loose ends dance, they spin and swirl,
Mismatched patterns, a colorful whirl.
Jokes are woven in every seam,
Wrapping the heart in a light-hearted dream.

A strand of folly, bright and wide,
Hiding giggles that can't abide.
We share our secrets, stitched with flair,
In every fold, a funny dare.

So let's unfurl this noisy yarn,
Embrace the wild and the less worn.
In every tear, a hearty cheer,
For life is comical, year after year.

Constellations in Threaded Skies

Stars are tangled, oh so bright,
In the fabric of the night.
Each twinkle tells a playful tale,
Of stitches gone awry, but won't pale.

A cosmic dance of zig and zag,
Life's a quilt, not just a rag.
Silly patterns, laughter shared,
In the milky way, our hearts are bared.

Threads that link this joyous spree,
Unexpected knots, wild and free.
With every laugh, a sparkling show,
In threads of gold, the truth will glow.

So here we drift on fabric's flow,
Celestial wraps, a cosmic row.
In constellations, we find our place,
As laughter weaves its soft embrace.

The Veil of Clarity

Behind the drape, a sight so clear,
A cat in a hat, oh dear, oh dear!
It sits on the couch with a royal air,
While plotting to steal all your comfy wear.

A wig on a broom, dancing by night,
Chasing the shadows, what a funny sight!
With giggles and whispers, it twirls with glee,
In a world where nothing makes sense to me.

A pair of old shoes that sport a grand grin,
Mumble sweet secrets, where to begin?
They tell of adventures and places far flung,
Of mischief and laughter, under moonlight sung.

Through curtains they peek, with eyes wide and bright,
Sneaking a look at the curious night.
With antics and jests, they flutter about,
In the veil of clarity, there's always a doubt.

Silken Permissions

In a world made of fabric, all wrinkled and bold,
A squirrel in a suit sipping tea, so bold!
It nods to the mirrors that giggle and wink,
Sipping opinions, with every sweet drink.

A monkey in slippers, checking the time,
Swings from the ceiling, oh isn't it prime?
Requests for permission, with utmost delight,
To jump on the table, 'cause why not tonight?

A walrus in sunglasses, lounging in style,
Counting his laughter for quite a while.
Unraveling secrets, each stitch tells a tale,
Of hats made of pudding, or tails like a whale.

When silk wraps around you, don't mind the laughs,
For every fine thread is a map of the gaffs.
In this playful world, let the silliness flow,
With silken permissions, let your humor glow!

Truths Entwined

In the garden of giggles, the blooms twist and shout,
Where gnomes play hopscotch and never pout.
They twirl in the sunshine, hats made of cheese,
Tickling each flower that dances with ease.

A parrot in pajamas claims it's a king,
Reciting long stories of nonsense and bling.
With feathers of rainbow that shimmer and shine,
He spills jokes and riddles like cheap, bubbly wine.

Weave all the tales of the cat and his cap,
With yarn made of laughter, it's all in the wrap.
For truth is a canvas of colors so bright,
In this fabric of fun, there's always delight.

So gather around and come witness the blend,
Of truths that are woven, and laughter that bends.
In a tapestry vibrant, with humor aligned,
Life's just a big joke, all truths intertwined.

Threads of Perception

Twisting and turning in circles absurd,
A llama in slippers has fully concurred.
Knitting strange patterns with yarn made of dreams,
Whispering secrets, oh how it redeems!

A fish in a sweater, just jiving along,
Singing old ballads, making us strong.
With fins made of velvet, oh what a twist,
In this land of the funny, how could we resist?

Each spool tells a joke, each thread holds a quip,
As comical visions dance, laugh, and skip.
The bridge of perception, so wobbly yet grand,
Will take you in circles through the laughter planned.

So come take a ride on this wild, funny ride,
With threads of perception where silliness hides.
Embrace every stitch, let the humor unfold,
In this world of deception, be wildly bold!

The Art of Unveiling

In a world of hides and seek,
Laughter drapes like silk so sleek.
What's under wraps, well, who can tell?
Maybe socks that rang a bell?

Peeling layers, oh what a show!
A jester's cap with a guffaw glow.
Is that a duck or just a sock?
All's fair when laughter takes stock!

Wraps so tight in woven cheer,
Turning whispers into a sneer.
What we wear, it's sometimes bold,
Underneath, truths can't be sold!

So let's unwind this spinning spree,
With giggles rising like a teehee.
Each uncoiled loop tells a tale,
Of silly truths that just won't pale!

Glimmers of Sincerity

In every jest, a sprinkle shines,
Truths disguised in playful lines.
A wink, a nod, a playful nudge,
Hiding secrets we'd misjudge.

Beneath bravado, sparks will dance,
Soft confessions in laughter's prance.
Who knew the punchline could reveal,
A heart so bright, a zest to feel?

Jokes may frolic, take their flight,
With undercurrents of delight.
Tangled webs of playful cheer,
Leading us to a truth quite clear.

Unmasking giggles, we will find,
The honest flakes that bliss remind.
In laughter's glow, sincerity,
Becomes the treasure, wild and free!

The Layered Affair

Beneath the frills, what lies in wait?
A sprinkle of humor, isn't it great?
Layers stacked, like a cake so sweet,
Each bite reveals a different treat.

With ribbons tied in knots of fun,
Every twist brings joy to run.
What's hidden deep, a comic gem,
In a bouquet of whimsy's hem.

Peeling back the feathered veil,
Finding truths that joke and flail.
A jester's grin, a tug of glee,
Inviting all to join the spree!

So let's indulge in this charade,
In layers thick, we won't evade.
Every chuckle, every cheer,
Unwraps the laughter we hold dear!

Threads Untwist

Threads of laughter start to sway,
Unravel secrets in a playful way.
With each tug, a giggle grows,
Tickling fiends where humor flows.

Loosening knots, oh what a sight,
Mirthful mischief takes to flight.
What will spring from silly threads?
Maybe a hat with berry spreads!

In woven tales where jests cascade,
Giggles blend in a vibrant parade.
As we untwist these crafty loops,
Truths peek out like playful poops!

So grab your needles, stitch with cheer,
Crafting joy in atmosphere.
With every twist and playful wink,
Laughter's truth, we will not sink!

Strung Narratives

In a room full of chatter, a tale begins,
One sock on the floor, where's the other twin?
A parrot in a hat, dancing on one foot,
Sips tea from a cup, a funny old brute.

The story unfolds with mismatched ends,
A cat with a tie, a dog that pretends.
Jokes get tangled, and laughter is found,
With each twist of fate, silliness abound.

A broomstick that flies, but only at night,
The ghosts in the attic, they study the light.
They giggle and scheme, hatching plans for the ball,
A waltz with a pumpkin, who's having a fall?

So here's to the plot, and all it can bear,
To all kinds of tales that wiggle and share.
In the land of the strange, we cheerfully play,
And dance with our quirks, in the silliest way.

Portraits of Error

A portrait so grand, but oh, what a sight,
With a nose like a pickle, and eyebrows that bite.
The artist is laughing, can barely move right,
As she paints with a flair that's both wrong and quite bright.

The frame's upside down, yet no one will care,
For the colors are wild, and the style's the flare.
With wigs on the dogs and mustaches on cats,
It's a charming display of whimsical chats.

Mistakes turn to magic, each blunder's a gem,
A face with three eyes, like a wobbly stem.
And yet, when you gaze, what peculiar delight,
Wit woven in strokes that will lighten the night.

So hang up the canvas, let laughter ignite,
With joyous oddities that feel just so right.
For life's a grand gallery, painted with jest,
We celebrate quirks, oh — it's simply the best!

Fabricated Luminescence

In a world made of bubbles, we float to the sky,
With cupcakes that giggle and clouds that can fly.
A flashlight that hiccups, it's hard to see straight,
As we stroll through the park on a magical date.

Each lantern a riddle, with shadows that dance,
A dragon that wiggles, caught up in a trance.
The stars change their colors from blue to bright green,
As we twirl with the fireflies, making a scene.

Our laughter erupts like confetti in air,
With glittery socks and a karaoke bear.
Sipping on noodles that twirl like a kite,
Every moment is silly, each heart feeling light.

So gather your friends for this brilliant parade,
In a realm full of giggles and joys that cascade.
For with every delight, we sparkle and gleam,
In a world full of whimsy, come live out the dream!

In the Tangle

A jumble of stories, a mess of good cheer,
With spaghetti that dances and fries with no fear.
The cat's in a tree with a weird rubber duck,
While the dog winks and grins, and runs out of luck.

A tangle of yarn, and it's all gone awry,
With a mouse on a skateboard, oh my, how they fly!
They sway through the room like a wacky parade,
As the chaos erupts, and the jokes all invade.

In this knotted-up world, it's hard to keep track,
Of the fun and the blunders that never fall flat.
With each twist we encounter, a chuckle shall grow,
As we weave through the fabric of laughter's warm glow.

So come join the fun, unravel your frown,
In the tangle of joy, silliness wears the crown.
For in every good twist, may it bring us a cheer,
In this playful old riddle, there's nothing to fear!

Braids of Perception and Clarity

In a knot of thoughts all tight,
Ideas twist, then take flight.
A braid of facts, a dash of jest,
Comedic truths put to the test.

With each turn, a giggle blooms,
Reality hops in quirky rooms.
Twists and turns, we laugh along,
In this chaos, we find our song.

Patterns shift, like socks on feet,
What's tangled up might taste like sweet.
A twisted tale, or maybe not,
In the end, it's all a plot.

So bring your quirks, your silly sides,
In this dance where humor hides.
With braids of perception, let laughter fly,
Even the serious can learn to try!

Unraveling the Golden Border

A thread of gold, what a sight,
Riddles wrapped in delight.
Pull a bit, watch it unfurl,
What secrets hide within this swirl?

Each tug reveals a funny thought,
A stitch of wisdom we all sought.
The edge of logic starts to fray,
In the mix, a playful play.

Chasing yarn, oh what a game,
A chase that's both folly and fame.
In tangled knots, we find our mirth,
The weirdness woven into our worth.

And as we laugh, let's be sincere,
A silly heart is why we're here.
Unraveling gold, with a twist or two,
In this tapestry, I find you!

Secrets in the Weft and Warp

Between the threads, so much to see,
A tapestry of quirky glee.
Woven tales in every seam,
Funny fables, a jovial dream.

Weft and warp, what a disguise,
Unexpected truths pop up like flies.
In the fabric of this playful lore,
You'll find secrets, and maybe more.

Every stitch a giggle grows,
In tangled yarn, humor flows.
With a snip and a snatch, cut it straight,
In the weaving, create your fate.

So let's embrace the oddball thread,
Laughing at what lies ahead.
For in the wefts, we can't ignore,
Life's hilarious, that's for sure!

The Dance of Shadows and Light

In shadows cast, a waltz unfolds,
Silly steps, as laughter holds.
A jig of joy beneath the sun,
Where funny moments come undone.

Light and dark, they spin around,
A quirky ballet, laughter found.
With each bend, a chuckle bright,
What a sight, this playful light.

Dance with flair, twirl with ease,
In the shadows, we tease and please.
With every step, a mishap's grace,
In this dance, we find our place.

So prance along, don't hold it tight,
In every shadow, find your light.
Let laughter reign as we share the stage,
In this delightful, fun-filled page.

Dappled Realms

In a land where fringes twirl and spin,
Colorful debates begin and grin.
Where ribbons argue who's more grand,
And laughter echoes across the land.

A pom-pom pranced with a goofy gait,
Claiming it's best, though it's just first-rate.
A feather scoffed, with a lofty air,
Saying, "You're fluff, I'm beyond compare!"

But what of the beads that jingle and sway?
They giggle low, joining the play.
For in this realm, the silliness reigns,
As all stitch tales with vibrant stains.

Echoes of Adornment

A bowtie snickered, slicked with pride,
While a necklace glanced, full of glitz, and wide.
Brushed gold and silver began to jest,
Competing for laughs, they both felt blessed.

In shadows, a brooch bursts, not shy at all,
Declaring a story, proud and tall.
As charms jingle-jangled, causing delight,
Each told their tale in the soft twilight.

With each gust of wind, colors would gleam,
Turning the mundane into a dream.
In this playful dance of bright and bold,
Every adornment has laughter to hold.

The Subtle Stitch

A single thread embarked on a quest,
To find a fabric that felt the best.
It traveled through seams, in hops and skips,
Telling tales of knots and funny quips.

A patch declared, "I'm quite the patch!"
While an applique replied, with a jazzy catch.
"You think you're cool, but I'm temperature high!"
Together they laughed, as fabric would fly.

Through stitches and nips, they formed a dance,
Every fold and tuck led to a chance.
For beneath every layer, a story was stitched,
In whispers of fabric, the world was bewitched.

Veils of Genuine

Behind a curtain of fabric and lace,
A hat tiptoed in a curious space.
Winking at shoes that sparkled and shone,
It gathered a crowd to share its own tone.

A scarf chimed in with a twist of the neck,
"My tales are better; I'm the captain of deck!"
But the boots just chuckled, feeling so wise,
"We all have our quirks, much to surprise."

As laughter erupted, they took center stage,
Each accessory played with a wit so sage.
In a world of fashion where humor ignites,
Every stitch and layer brings joyful delights.

Dainty Contrasts

Frills and flair dance in the sun,
A wiggle here, a twirl just for fun.
Dressed to impress, yet all a guise,
Behind the lace, the truth often lies.

In high heels wobbling, they take a stand,
Claiming elegance, as if it's planned.
But trip they do, and oops! Down they go,
A laugh erupts; oh, what a show!

Sequins gleam, a dazzling display,
While the heart plays in a playful way.
With every twirl, each twinkle bright,
The mirror reflects what feels just right.

Yet beneath the layers, where mishaps breed,
It's all a charade—oh yes indeed!
With smiles we wear until the night,
For in the end, it's all delight.

The Costumed Reality

Oh, the hats we wear in this big parade,
Each character crafted, none are afraid.
With capes and cloaks, we strut with flair,
Behind these smiles, do we truly care?

The jester's laugh, the wizard's spell,
City folk think they know it well.
But peeking through costumes, oh what a sight!
It's just me in pajamas, lost in the night!

Masks on our faces, a playful deceit,
Who's really brave when we face the street?
Underneath the colors and fabrics bright,
A tale spins on—take flight, take flight!

As the curtain falls, we shed the game,
But isn't it fun to bask in fame?
With a wink and a grin, we bow to the crowd,
For when it's all over, we laugh out loud!

Cords of Perception

Tangled strings in a joyful mess,
Pull one here, find the very best.
Knotted thoughts and twisted seams,
Reality isn't quite what it seems.

With every tug, a giggle spills,
As we weave through life, we've got the skills.
A puppet show without a string,
In the chaos, the laughter sings!

Perceptions shift like a playful breeze,
Chasing the truth with giggly ease.
The more we tug, the more we see,
A dance of viewpoints, wild and free!

So spin the tale and pull the thread,
In the comedy of life, no tears to shed.
With each knot tied, we wear a grin,
Life's tangled cord spills joy within!

Shiny Facades

A shiny shell on a cracked-up core,
Glittering smiles—but what's in store?
With every sparkle, a backstory hides,
Where laughter lives and cringe resides.

Glossy layers of laughter they take,
But inside the sparkle, we often shake.
Beneath the gloss, the cue cards read,
'Act like you're fine, it's all you need!'

With winks and nods, they play their role,
Masked in gleeful art, what a toll!
For when the night brings shadows near,
The silence speaks more than any cheer.

So shine away with a wink and pose,
For laughter's the way, we all know it grows.
Through the shiny facades, let joy unfurl,
As we twirl our way in this funny world!

Embroidered Whispers

In a world where threads can speak,
Adventures grow with every peak.
Stitches tell tales of every cheer,
While mishaps dance, the end is near.

Frogs in hats and cats in pants,
We giggle wild at their strange prance.
Needles hum a merry tune,
As fabrics laugh beneath the moon.

Patterns swirl in colors bright,
Accurate lies bring sheer delight.
Each twist and turn, a jest to make,
Those hidden truths, do take a break.

So let the seams bring joy and glee,
In every stitch, a mystery.
For when we sew and when we play,
The funny side will always stay.

The Weave of Honesty

In a room where fabric sways,
A tapestry of wittier days.
With every thread, a truth might bend,
But laughter's charm will never end.

Woven tales of socks mismatched,
Crinkled shirts and frames detached.
With a flick, the humor shows,
As wardrobes hide their little woes.

Beneath the seams, a secret lies,
Like a duck that thinks it flies.
Each twist reveals an honest jest,
In silly ways, we feel the best.

So spin those threads with joy and glee,
In every snag, delight will be.
For honesty, when worn with flair,
Is the funniest style that we bear.

Adorned Deceptions

A jacket claims it's purest silk,
But really it's made of cow's milk.
Fancy ties speak of great designs,
But some are stuck with grapevine twines.

Hats perched high, with feathers blue,
Whisper secrets, none quite true.
Each button lies with playful winks,
The fashion truth, a jest, it thinks.

Patterns mix with silly flair,
With clashing socks that fill the air.
Each garment giggles, can you hear?
In this grand ball, it's all sincere.

So while we dress with all our might,
Let laughter be the guiding light.
For what we wear, though jesting too,
Is but a mask for all we do.

Strands of Insight

In every thread, a twist to find,
Each colorful yarn is intertwined.
The fabric laughs, the colors boast,
Its comical charm we love the most.

With every pull of yarn so bright,
We unravel truths both wrong and right.
Cleverly sewn with a wink and grin,
These whispers glide, let humor in.

A patchwork quilt of oddities,
Whirling tales in pastimes' breeze.
Knots and loops don't always match,
Yet wisdom glimmers in every patch.

So let's embrace this colorful game,
Where threads of laugh become our fame.
For in this weave, so wild and free,
Humor reigns, as it should be.

Revealing the Lattice of Life

In the corners of reality, things get a bit tight,
Knots and loops dance, oh what a sight!
Like shoelaces tangled, trying to behave,
Life's a game of hopscotch, at least it's a rave.

Threads of bright laughter weave through the air,
Jokes float like feathers, light as a prayer.
Every mishap a stitch, every giggle a seam,
In the fabric of folly, we all dare to dream.

With patterns of chaos, we waddle and sway,
Woven together, we brighten the day.
From frayed edges and giggles, we pull and we tug,
Life's riveting tapestry gives us a hug.

Oh, how we prance through this colorful maze,
Laughing at limps and quirky displays.
In the fabric of laughter, we flourish and play,
The lattice we tread on never leads us astray.

Fringe Benefits of Being Real

Life's a parade, with feathers and flair,
Dressed in a costume, with nary a care.
Swapping the serious for a silly charade,
We dance through the truth in a funky cascade.

The edges of honesty fray like a thread,
With quirks and oddities regularly spread.
Being genuine brings giggles and cheer,
Embracing the madness that we all hold dear.

Juggling our blunders like ripe, juicy fruit,
The joy of the awkward is oh so acute.
With humor we stitch our best moments in place,
Each laugh a reminder, we've got style and grace.

So tip your hat to the funny and free,
In this glorious chaos, let's all just agree.
The fringe that we flaunt makes us beautifully real,
Woven with laughter, oh what a good deal!

The Tapestry of Unspoken Thoughts

In shadows and whispers, ideas take flight,
Threads of the mind blend dark with the light.
Silence has stories, they bubble and swirl,
As unspoken giggles around us unfurl.

Like a loom at its dance, thoughts twist and they turn,
Each yarn a secret we laugh and we learn.
Connecting the particles, we skip and we hop,
Creating a quilt with a whimsical top.

A tapestry vibrant, in colors so bold,
Unraveling stories that dare to be told.
With a wink and a smile, we fashion the scheme,
In the realm of the quiet, we dare to dream.

So let's weave our moments, a fabric of cheer,
Where the loudness of silence is sweetly sincere.
In the tapestry woven, let giggles have sway,
For unspoken laughter means we're here to stay.

Glimmers Behind the Gossamer

In the soft glow of whispers, secrets collide,
Life's little quirks hide where shadows reside.
Behind strands of laughter, the truth plays a game,
Unraveling joy that's just never the same.

A web of reflections, oh isn't it grand?
Each twinkle a tale spun from fairyland.
Through the gossamer layers, we all take a peek,
Glimmers of nonsense make hearts feel unique.

Between grids of giggles, we find our own way,
A dance of absurdity brightens the day.
Step into the shimmer, it's quirky and bright,
Where laughter will guide us, in day or in night.

So let's polish our sparkle, embrace the bizarre,
With glimmers of laughter, we'll travel so far.
Behind all the layers, our true selves will shine,
In the tapestry woven of joy so divine.

Adornments of Authenticity

With glitter here and ribbons there,
We flaunt our stuff—a show with flair.
Yet underneath this vibrant show,
Are secrets hiding, or so they glow.

In garish beads and bright confetti,
We dance around like cats—so petty.
A wink, a smile, we keep it light,
With feathery quirks that feel just right.

Jokes on us, in awkward grace,
As we twirl about, a funny race.
Each quip a fabric, sewn so tight,
Unraveling truths in sheer delight.

So here's to frills and jests galore,
Mismatched joy in endless store.
Beneath the bling, we find our cheer,
A merry laugh—our truth is clear.

Silken Whispers of Revelation

In whispers soft, the ribbons lay,
With every twist, they seem to sway.
A secret spun in colors bright,
What's really there? It's quite a sight!

The clink of charms upon our shoes,
Signal stories we might refuse.
Yet at each turn, we trip and fall,
Tangled tales, we laugh through all!

Silk slips out from every seam,
Revealing how we like to dream.
So pull a thread, see what you find,
A knot of jokes, we're all entwined.

In this parade of patchwork fun,
What's really us? The quest's begun!
A chuckling truth wrapped nice and tight,
In silken laughs, we find our light.

Frayed Edges of Existence

With frayed edges, we strut and prance,
In mismatched socks, we take our chance.
Oh what a sight, this ragged crew,
With every misstep, we start anew!

Like threads that dangle, how they sway,
In life's big tapestry, come what may.
We giggle loud when we trip and fall,
The truest tales, they fill the hall.

Each stitch a mischief, each knot a prank,
In life's wild quilt, we simply tank.
But check your pockets—what's that delight?
A treasure trove of giggles, light!

So raise a toast to all our flaws,
For in the rags, we find our cause.
With frayed edges, we'll craft our fate,
And laugh at life, it's sure a plate!

Strands of Sincerity Untangled

In tangled strands of vibrant hue,
We spin our wheels, but it's all true.
Each loop a laugh, each twist a grin,
In this wild ride, we're bound to win!

With shiny baubles, we show our style,
Yet underneath, we feign a wile.
As truth peeks through the vibrant threads,
We giggle soft at what life spreads.

The punchlines hide in nooks of flair,
Every truth draped with a bit of air.
What's real? Who knows? We play our part,
In this great circus, we're all art.

So let's untangle these witty ropes,
With every snag, we nurture hopes.
In strands of fun, we dance and cheer,
For life's a jest, our hearts sincere!

The Tangled Narrative

In a world of threads and cheer,
The tales we weave are far from clear.
Buttons pop and seams unwind,
Laughter echoes, oh how fun to find!

Stitching stories, wild and free,
With needle and thread, it's comedy!
Patterns clash like socks in pairs,
A wardrobe's worth of jokes and snares.

Fabric swirls, a carnival scene,
Where truth hides behind the sheen.
We wear our quirks, a frayed display,
In a jumbled fashion, come what may!

So gather 'round, let's knit our dreams,
In tangled threads and endless themes.
For in the mess, the giggles burst,
A joyful fabric, where laughter's first!

Woven Affections

In knit and purl, our heartstrings play,
With every loop, we dance and sway.
A patchwork quilt of love that's rare,
   Yet in its seams, we lose a hair!

Odd socks sit in mismatched glee,
Five yarns later, where could they be?
Knots of humor, tangled tight,
   A cozy corner full of light!

We fashion ties from jest and glee,
With every stitch, we just can't see.
A scarf that wraps in jumbled grace,
   Leaves us laughing, just in case!

So snip the thread of worry's plight,
Embrace the chaos, it feels so right.
With woven hearts and silly spins,
Life's fabric shimmers, the laughter wins!

The Truth in Fabric

Beneath the layers, tales unfold,
In patches bright, the stories told.
A hem that's crooked, a button gone,
In tangled truth, it rolls along.

Fabrics mix like oddball friends,
Their antics loud, the laughter blends.
A costume party gone askew,
With polka dots and plaid in view!

Behind the seams, the chuckles grow,
In folds of fabric, silliness flows.
A cloak of joy, a cape of cheer,
We wear our giggles, year by year!

So stitch your tales with threads of light,
In every fold, find sheer delight.
For life's a fabric, free and bold,
In laughter's warmth, the truth is gold!

Adrift in Decor

In a room adorned with quirky flair,
We giggle at the oddball pair.
Framed art that's crooked, just like my hat,
A splash of color, oh imagine that!

Curtains dancing in a jolly breeze,
With monkeys on the wall, if you please.
Pillows fighting for a comfy spot,
A funny mix, we love a lot!

Amidst the chaos, where laughter sings,
Every detail a surprise it brings.
A vase that's chipped, a rug that's wild,
This merry space, both fun and styled!

So let's adorn with whimsy's grip,
And sail through life on a decor trip.
For every chuckle, every cheer,
Is woven into the love we steer!

The Complexity of Color

In hues of fuchsia, I found my socks,
They danced on walls like sly little rocks.
The lemon crayon, it giggles and sways,
While smelly markers have colorful days.

In splashes of teal, my breakfast appears,
Pancakes with sprinkles, oh, what a cheers!
The forest is blue, with a manga-like grin,
As purple trees whisper, 'Let's do it again!'

A rainbow confetti in a jumbled mess,
Wanna color my hair? I guess, I confess!
With color so bold, life takes a new spin,
But dogs still look puzzled, where do I begin?

So let's paint our world with all the right shades,
A canvas of giggles, where mischief parades!
In this artful mess, joy's easy to find,
Color your laughter, let colors unwind!

Interlaced Whispers

In twirls and sways, the echoes do play,
Chasing secrets in a curious way.
One whispers softly, 'What shall we do?'
While another retorts, 'Let's wear something blue!'

Oh, the tales that the shadows can weave,
Like socks in a dryer, oh, who can believe?
A giggling breeze steals my hat from my head,
It flutters away—how dare it, I said!

Two cats in a tangle, they plan a grand scheme,
To steal every cookie, to shatter my dream.
But I laugh at their paws, oh so adorably sly,
As they slyly conspire while I bake apple pie.

With laughter entwined in the fabric of night,
These interlaced whispers bring sheer delight.
So let's dance with shadows, let's weave and let go,
In the magical chaos, let giggles all flow!

Charmed Mysteries

In a box of old charms, all jumbled and bright,
Lies a rubber chicken that giggles at night.
A spoon that can whistle, a hat that will sing,
All tales in my treasure, each charm's got a zing!

A mirror that grins when I'm feeling quite blue,
And a pumpkin that dreams of being a shoe.
As I sift through this mess, what a curious sight,
Each charm tells a story, hilariously right!

Mysteries linger in every small trinket,
Like socks in a drawer, oh, which one do I pick?
The trolls toss their glitter, oh let's have a ball,
In this charmed little world, we giggle through all.

So here's to our secrets, we'll keep them untold,
In laughter we'll grow, together, be bold!
An enchanted adventure where joy is the key,
With charming oddities, just you wait and see!

Shimmering Facades

A fountain of glitter spills over the street,
And cats wearing top hats engage in a feat.
With sparkles and giggles, the landscape's so bright,
You can't help but chuckle at every small sight.

In mirrors of laughter, reflections are keen,
Where ducks wear bowties and ice cream is green.
The trees whisper secrets in a twirling waltz,
While snowflakes do pirouettes, no need for a vault!

Each corner conceals a new charming display,
Like taffy that dances or gumdrops at play.
Where sincerity merges with whimsical flair,
In this shimmering world, laughter fills the air.

So let's toast to figments, so crazy yet grand,
As we skip through the moments with joy at our hand.
In the entangled effulgence, let's twirl and embrace,
These shimmering facades create a magical space!

The Fabric of Hidden Stories

In a world where fibers twist,
The truth often takes a tryst.
With every stitch a tale unfolds,
Of secrets wrapped in gossamer gold.

The seams may fray, the colors clash,
Yet laughter dances with each bash.
Beneath the cloth, a jest is spun,
Life's fabric weaves a playful pun.

From tiny knots to patterns wide,
We hide our truths like bugs that slide.
The fabric whispers, 'What a show!'
As neighbors squint and glance below.

So wear your quilt of tales so bright,
Each patch a giggle, pure delight.
And should they ask what's sewn, you'll grin,
For lies and laughs are stitched within.

Loomed Lies

In the corner sits a loom so grand,
Tangled lies on each strand.
With fingers crossed and eyes a-wink,
We weave the stories—never think.

Each thread a tale of what's been said,
Some truths flew off and others bled.
A feather here, a dust mote there,
We spin the yarn with crafty flair.

Oh, the bobbins spin with laughter,
As we chase down "happily ever after."
A fabric forged with humor bright,
Creates a cloak to hide from sight.

Each knot we tie, a chuckle shared,
In this loomed dance, we're never scared.
For when the fibers start to fray,
We tell another whopper, come what may!

Woven Dreams

In dreams we weave a tale so sweet,
A fabric dance on whimsical feet.
Each thread a wish, a giggle, a sigh,
As we stitch hopes beneath the sky.

From moonlit nights to sunny days,
Our canvas flows in merry ways.
The joyous knots tie us in glee,
As we giggle at life's tapestry.

Oh, the shapes of dreams can twist and twine,
With every loop, oh what a sign!
A creature here, a dance so fine,
We laugh at fate, for life's a line.

In each woven stitch, we find our way,
Through laughter's maze, we dance and play.
So let the fibers take their flight,
For woven dreams bring pure delight!

Shimmering Signposts of Verity

Shiny signs on the road we tread,
With glimmers of truth, by laughter led.
Each twinkling spark, a wink from fate,
As we navigate this funny state.

The paths we stroll have twists and turns,
And lessons learned are what we yearn.
With every step, a chuckle flows,
The shimmer grows as merriment glows.

Our signposts gleam with stories bold,
Of whispers 'round the fires controlled.
With every ray of sunlight's beam,
We giggle at what the fables seem.

So raise the banner, let laughter reign,
Through shimmering truths that tease the brain.
We wander in glee through life's absurdity,
With shining signs of humor's clarity!

Colorful Threads of Deception

A vibrant palette spills on the floor,
With threads of color, tales galore.
Each hue a hint of mischief bright,
As we spin yarns into the night.

The red is anger, yet makes us laugh,
While blue suggests a comical gaff.
A rainbow mix, we stitch and weave,
In vibrant tales, we all believe.

With crafty hands, we paint our lies,
As giggles dance through sparkling skies.
The fabric glows with every seam,
In this parade of a playful dream.

So grab the threads, let's make a mess,
With colors wild, it's all excess.
For in this quilt of pure pretense,
We find our joy, we find our sense.

www.ingramcontent.com/pod-product-compliance
Lightning Source LLC
Chambersburg PA
CBHW070002300426
43661CB00141B/153